Printed in PRC
First Printing, 2018

Published and Distributed by
Freedom International Publishing
Gibsonton, FL

Titles may be purchased in bulk. For information, please email
Ashley@thekeeperofmyheart.com

The Keeper of My Heart

www.thekeeperofmyheart.com

Cover and book design by Laura Sebold, Lesebold@gmail.com
Illustrations by Laura Sebold and from istockphoto.com

Note to reader: This work is never to replace The Holy Bible. It is merely a depiction of what the author believes the heart of Jesus is speaking to his daughters of all ages in all countries.

The Keeper of My Heart

The Keeper of My Heart is dedicated to YOU, the one holding this book. May you find your true worth and confidence in the One who holds your heart and in the One who longs to hear from the real you...the you that Jesus loves unconditionally.

I pray that you are set free through discovering the truth of how Jesus sees you, and that this truth dispels all the lies you have believed about yourself.

May you be inspired to be all that He says you are!

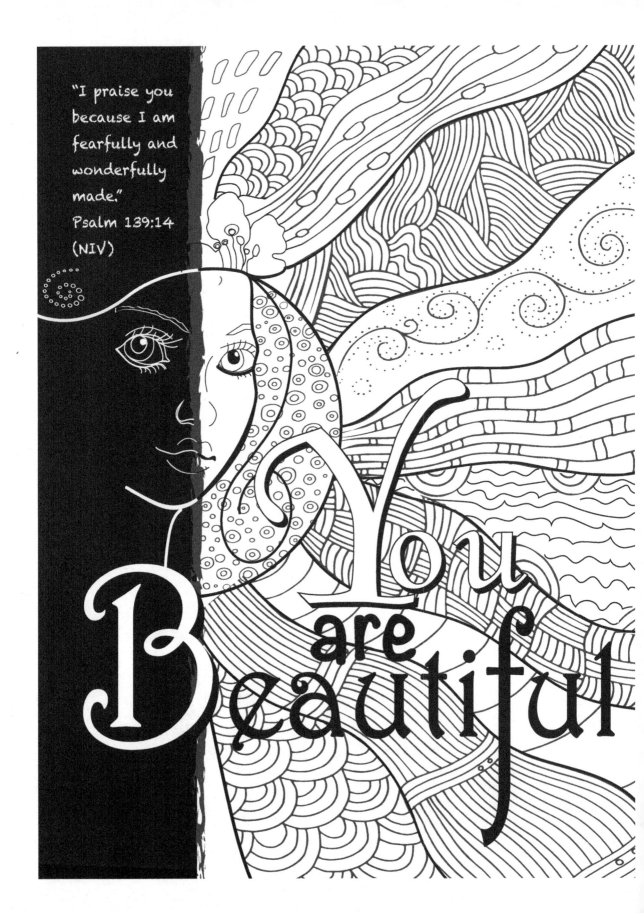

"I praise you because I am fearfully and wonderfully made."
Psalm 139:14 (NIV)

You are Beautiful

Hi Beautiful,

Yes, I said beautiful because you are! You are an amazing creation, beautifully and wonderfully made. And you were made on purpose! It is no mistake that you are alive and reading this book right now.

You see, you are an actual work of art, a masterpiece, which means you are completely unique with a special mind, body, and soul. Your physical appearance was given with careful thought.

Consider for a moment that you are an amazing artist and you created the most beautiful painting, one that could never be copied or duplicated because it's an original done by you. This painting is rare, so rare that no one could actually buy it. All of a sudden, a stranger walks up and takes a paintbrush and changes a few things because, in their opinion, it "looks better."

How insulting and awful would that be if you were the artist? An original, a beautifully and wonderfully made painting, changed because of an opinion of someone else.

Oh, beautiful girl, that is what you do when you compare yourself, your face, and your body to what you see on television or to what someone else thinks is beautiful. You are wishing away the very things that were carefully considered. You are your Heavenly Father's beloved creation. He is proud of you. I am proud of you.

As difficult as this may be, I want you to go look at yourself in the mirror and say, "I am beautifully and wonderfully made. I embrace who I am and who I was created to be. I am special and my maker thinks I am perfectly put together. Every morning he says to me, 'Good morning, beautiful.'"

I love you, your beauty, your personality, and your soul.

Love,
The keeper of your heart

"I am jealous for you with a godly jealousy..." 2 Corinthians 11:2 (NIV)

"And I will make you my promised bride forever. I will be good and fair. I will show you my love and mercy." Hosea 2:19 (ICB)

You are Loved

My Love,

Do you have ANY idea how much I love you? Do you know that I love you so much that I will NEVER LEAVE YOU?

My love is so much more than anyone's love for you. It's COMPLETE. You see, when I give my heart ... it's FOREVER. You can be sure of that. You never have to worry that I "don't love you anymore" or that anything you've done in the past or anything you do in the future will make me love you less. My love is perfectly WHOLE. I do not ever give my heart in pieces; it's my whole heart I give to you without any regret or restraint.

I will prove to you how much I love you.

Over 2,000 years ago, long before you were born, I willingly laid down my life for all of your past sin and your future sin. I gave up my life even BEFORE you knew me, so that you could be FREE of the punishment of sin, and be WITH ME in my Father's house for eternity. I did it, praying that you would accept my love, and in return give me YOUR heart.

I know that you can't love me the same way that I love you, but in time, as you see me CONSISTENTLY loving you, your love will grow deeper and deeper for me. And this excites me! You falling more in love with me makes me smile so big. Just knowing the possibilities of what our relationship can be brings me so much joy!

You are loved by the King of all kings!

My darling, the best love stories and your favorite romantic movies have NOTHING on the love that I have for you. If you can tune into my presence in your life, you will begin to see that I am actually the lover of your SOUL. Yes, your soul, the thing that makes you the most unique, beautiful girl that you are. I am the one romancing your soul and I will show you what true love is.

When you do come to understand what TRUE LOVE is, you won't settle for the warped love that the world has to give you, or the kind of love that someone wants to give you that doesn't portray MY love for you.

When the purity of my love opens your eyes so wide, and you realize how I value you, and how worthy you are of perfect love, you will finally begin to value your own soul. This awakening will change your life forever. It will keep you from making choices that will damage your heart and leave you with devastating soul wounds. This kind of awakening will direct you to make decisions that are healthy for your mind, body, and soul.

My love, will you give me your heart? You already have all of mine. I am right next to you waiting for you to put your hand in mine.

Yours truly,
The keeper of your heart

_____

_____

_____

_____

_____

_____

_____

"I, even I, am he who blots out your transgressions, for my own sake, and remembers your sins no more."
Isaiah 43:25 (NIV)

"He has taken our sins away from us as far as the east is from west."
Psalm 103:12 (ICB)

My Precious One,

When I look at you, I don't see what you see.

I see a beautiful girl, dressed in white, who is clean from the inside, pure in heart. I see you and what broke your heart, and I am right now, in this moment, gathering those pieces together to make it whole.

I see you, not what you've done.

I see your heart's intentions, not the actions you regret.

I see your beauty, not what you think is ugly.

When I look at you, I don't think about all the things you've asked forgiveness for. Simply because all of that was already paid in full!

When I look at you, I see your future, your healing, you smiling with joy because I have made you new.

When I look at you, all the wrongs have been made right, and you are like a beautiful, precious bride waiting for her groom in a delicate, white dress.

I see you, and I am waiting in anticipation for our next adventure together, the moment you will realize that I love you, that I am really with you, and that NOTHING separates you from my love.

When I look at you, I say, "Let go of the past, my darling. It doesn't matter; what matters is now. Let me heal you and make you new, let me build you back into the amazing girl you are supposed to be."

When I see you, I can't wait for you to look back at me and say, "I say yes to you. I say yes to your healing and yes to your promises. Build me into the person that my destiny is waiting for."

Will you say yes?

I love you with my whole heart.

Love,
The keeper of yours

_____

_____

_____

_____

_____

_____

_____

_____

"...Whoever touches you touches the apple of his eye-" Zechariah 2:8 (NIV)

You Are Worthy

To the Apple of My Eye,

I would climb the highest mountain and go to the lowest part of the Earth to get to your heart, to have just a moment where we meet and I get to share my love for you.

I go wherever you go, even to the places I don't belong, and it is there that I have shown you my undying love for you. It is because you are worthy and I want you to know your worth.

Somewhere on your journey, you believed a lie that your worth was found in something that it's NOT. Do you remember that moment? I do. I was right there with you, and my heart ached with pain when you believed a lie that has tried to steal your destiny, your joy, your peace, your reason for living.

Since that moment, I have shown you my love in many ways, competing for your attention, but your eyes would never quite focus on me enough to see the TRUTH. Now that your eyes are focusing, let me tell you the truth:

Your worth is not in your body.

Your worth is not in how you look, how cute you are, how pretty your hair is, or how skinny you are.
Your worth is not in how much money you have.
Your worth is not in who your family is.
Your worth is not in what you do for other people.
Your worth is not in how smart you are.
Your worth is not in where you live.
Your worth is not in how you talk.
Your worth is not in the stuff you have.
Your worth is not in the good things you've done or the ugly things you've done.
Your worth is not in what you've given away.
Your worth is not in a talent.
Your worth is not in the opinions of others.
Your worth is not in the way another person looks at you.

Your worth, your true value, is in your SOUL, the one I gave my life for.
Pause and think about that for a moment.
Is it possible that you have been focused on things that have nothing to do with your value at all? When you put your worth in anything other than me, it will actually lead to you feeling worth less than your true value.

Put aside the many things you have thought your worth comes from, and instead put that energy and focus on me, the lover of your soul, the one who can make you feel worthy of love, beauty, and the best life.
Because YOU are worthy of it.

Love,
The keeper of your heart

_____

_____

_____

_____

_____

_____

_____

_____

"Trust in the Lord with all your heart and lean not on your own understanding; in all your ways submit to him, and he will make your paths straight."
Proverbs 3:5-6 (NIV)

My Sweetheart,

In the moments when you feel weak, emotional, and tired of the circumstances of life. I am still with you. Lean on me. Picture yourself resting your head on my big shoulder and me holding you up with my strength.

I know all about the things in life that you don't understand, and you ask me, "why is this happening?" I know you wonder if there will ever be an answer. Believe this: THROUGH IT ALL, you are STRONG IN ME!

Let my strength complete you when you are weak and tired. I desire that you rest in knowing that I will take care of you, that you lay your head on my shoulder and entrust your troubles to me.

When you truly trust me, I will make you soar on wings of eagles above your troubles. I will give you peace in the storm, and I will give you strength! Strength to keep trusting, strength to keep going, and strength to overcome. You WILL get through these trials in your life and you will grow stronger because of them if you CHOOSE to lean on me.

You can't always see that I am continually working things into a pattern of good in your life, but if you choose to walk WITH ME in this life, you will look back and see how I delivered you and took care of you to help you reach a place of peace.

I will not fail you.

I love you.

Love,
The keeper of your heart

"For those who find me find life and receive favor from the Lord." Proverbs 8:35 (NIV)

YOU are FAVORED

My Beautiful Girl,

What are your dreams? The dreams deep down in your heart. What is it that you truly want in your life? Close your eyes and think about it for a minute.

I LONG to fulfill your dreams. I want to give you those deepest desires, the dreams you think you could never actually attain. Those are what I want to give to you – in the right time.

The life that you've been given, my darling, is a journey, a journey of becoming the "true you" that you were created to be.

On this journey, I will be with you, giving you favor on each step of the way as long as you STEP WITH ME.

Sometimes, yes, you may have to take a step when you aren't sure if I am there or not, but my gentle hand is right there to guide you in the better direction. The KEY is to be WILLING to follow me.

Because of me, you have favor with the Father, and the Scripture says that when your eyes are on me, you will have the desires of your heart. Please remember that I love you enough NOT to give you something that's bad for you.

With anything that you do in life, when you look away is when a mishap occurs. Think about driving: Keep your eyes on the road and you won't veer off the path. It's the same way with me.

When you keep your eyes on me and consider me, ask me, and talk to me about your relationships, problems at school, and future jobs – and it is your desire to do right – I will LEAD you to the areas of FAVOR that I have planned for you.

If you will place every single thing you have in your life, including the dreams in your heart, in my strong and powerful hands, I will take it all and make what is supposed to be. I will bring you to your destiny!

Do you trust me? Will you listen to my lead when you know in your heart the answer is "no"? Because I will tell you this: If the answer is NO, that means there is an even greater YES that lies ahead.

I am so captivated by you and I love so much to hear your heart speak to mine.

Will you tell me your dreams? Will you tell me what you desire even now?

I am listening ...

Love,
The keeper of your heart

_____

_____

_____

_____

_____

_____

_____

_____

_____

_____

_____

_____

_____

_____

_____

"Then you will know the truth, and the truth will set you free."
John 8:32
(NIV)

You Are FREE

"Now the Lord is the Spirit, and where the Spirit of the Lord is, there is freedom."
2 Corinthians 3:17 (NIV)

"So if the Son sets you free, you will be free indeed."
John 8:36 (NIV)

My Love,

YOU ARE FREE:
- free of fear – my name has power;
- free of guilt – there is no condemnation in me;
- free of the punishment of sin – I took it for you!
- free to be YOU – I love the REAL you;
- free to worship me – I am so proud of you, be proud to worship me;
- free to pursue your dreams – with me you can do ALL things;
- free from death – you will live in eternity with me;
- free to choose – it's a gift in this life, choose what's right;
- free of the law – you don't have to earn my love, you already have it;
- free from worry – trust me, I have ALL that you need. I am your provider;
- free from offense – forgive quickly as I have forgiven you and you also will be free from bitterness.

True freedom comes only from knowing me, understanding my love for you, and believing what I have done for you.

The deeper you fall in love with me, the more freedom you will gain. You will have freedom from pain deep in your heart because I will speak healing into your life. You will have freedom from what others think of you because you will care more about what I think of you. But it all starts with me.

Walk with me daily and dwell on truth because, my love, the TRUTH is what SETS YOU FREE!

Love,
The keeper of your heart

"And since we are his children, we are his heirs. In fact, together with Christ we are heirs of God's glory..."
Romans 8:17 (NLT)

You are Royalty

Dear Princess,

Where is your crown? Why did you put it down when you were a little girl? I LOVED watching you act like a princess and try on your pretty slippers, curtsy, and dance – you were confident and felt in your heart the royalty that you are.

I have watched how the world and the ugliness of it took that confidence and innocence away, but today you are going to pick your crown back up!

You are a princess, beautiful girl! You have royalty in the blood running through your veins if you have accepted me into your heart.

This means that YOU are the daughter of THE KING. You, my princess, are of great value.

A princess whose father is the king does not accept disrespect. She knows her value and does not need another person to "accept" her to make her feel loved. A princess is a noble young lady who carries herself with poise and dignity. She is respectful, listening to the voice of the king, and choosing her words wisely.

A princess is brave because she knows the king and his entire army backs her up! She doesn't fear the future, but embraces life and chases her dreams.

A princess is PROUD of her royalty and proud of the king, and the king is proud of her.

A princess knows that the king would do anything for her, and she enjoys the love he lavishes on her.

A princess has courage to stand up against evil and turns wrongs into rights.

A princess truly knows her value because of her bloodline, and she is careful not to be in the wrong place at the wrong time for the enemy to steal anything from her.

YOU are a princess! YOU are a daughter of the KING! Because I live in your heart, you now reign with me!

It's time to start acting like the royalty that you are.

Pick up your crown, place it on your head, and look in the mirror and say, "I am a true princess, a daughter of the king. I am not moved by the world for my God and king is with me."

Love,
The keeper of your heart

P.S. If you have not yet asked me to live in your heart, turn to the letter titled "Heavenbound".

_____

_____

_____

_____

_____

_____

"God's loyal
love couldn't
have run out,
his merciful
love couldn't
have dried up.
They're created
new every
morning. How
great your
faithfulness...
God proves to
be good to
the man who
passionately
waits, to the
woman who
diligently
seeks."
Lamentations
3:23-25
(MSG)

You
Are
New

To My Beloved,

Today you are NEW, yesterday is old – along with the negative things attached to it. All of those yesterdays do not even exist anymore. What is real are the present moment and the future I have for you.

With each new day, my mercies are new! That means that with each new sunrise comes an opportunity to START OVER, not looking back, but only looking forward.

I know it's hard to forget the old memories that are there, but they only exist in your mind. Let me help you break free from those memories.

As you are beginning to see what I see in you and what I created you to be, you will feel more and more distant from the life that once was. My presence in and around you will make those memories seem as if they were another life, another person, because you won't relate to them anymore. This will allow free rein to become your true self.

At first, it will be difficult to not look back. But as your mind gets stronger, you will refuse those thoughts and refuse the memories, and eventually begin to thank me for bringing you out of the pit. The more you see yourself in me, the further apart you will grow from the past... until one day you literally smile and feel joy in your heart because of how far you've come.

Focus on the present moment and this new day, which is an opportunity to become aligned with me, with my words, and with the truth of who you are. Let go of the past! You are NEW.

Love,
The keeper of your heart

"This I declare about the Lord: He alone is my refuge, my place of safety; he is my God, and I trust him."
Psalm 91:2 (NLT)

You are Safe

My Darling,

You are safe with me. I will never hurt you. I will never insult you. I will only love you and care for you unlike anyone you have ever known. It is my heart's desire that you come to me like a child and cast all your burdens upon me, and allow me to be that someone who listens without judgment or ridicule. I LONG to hear EVERYTHING you go through EVERY day. Tell me what troubles you. Tell me what makes you happy. Tell me your dreams. Tell me what you think you need. Tell me what confuses you.

You are precious to me, and your thoughts and feelings are safe with me. I am here to listen and to lean on, and it is not a burden for me to listen to what's on your heart and mind like it might be for others. There is NO LIMIT to the thoughts and emotions you can share with me, and there is no time limit, either.

Talk, write, draw, cry, yell, laugh ... with me.

I am the keeper of your heart, and you are safe with me.

Love,
The keeper of your heart

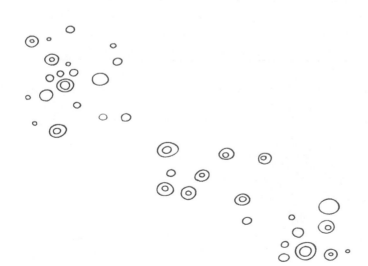

"When I am filled with cares, your comfort brings me joy."
Psalm 94:19 (HCSB)

YOU ARE JOYFUL

"Now may the God of hope fill you with all joy and peace as you believe in Him so that you may overflow with hope by the power of the Holy Spirit."
Romans 15:13 (HCSB)

Dear Sunshine,

Do you know how much I love to see you smile and laugh? It brings me such joy to see you happy. I know that your mind is full of "stuff," like worries, doubts, and fears, but your brain was actually designed for you to be full of joy!

You were created not to worry about tomorrow, but to live in the present moment, enjoying life.

If you can hand over to me the things that consume your mind and allow yourself to come into agreement with the truth, that I will bring you through each difficulty in life and make you stronger, it's then that you create ROOM for the joy in your heart to arise.

When you are sad and depressed about something, come to me and cry – cry hard if you have to, letting out your built-up emotions, and lay it down at my feet in trust. Once you have left it at my feet, don't allow yourself to think negatively. When you see yourself going in that direction, pause to remind yourself that you have placed that something with me, and then fix your mind on a POSITIVE thing. Doing this makes room in your mind for joy. It makes me happy to see you joyful, and that is why I said to cast your cares on ME.

YOU were never meant to carry your burdens!

I came so that you might have an abundant life, which includes abundant joy! This joy comes from hope and anticipation of the good plans I have for you, knowing that your relationship with your Creator is growing, and believing in the promise that I will make a beautiful painting of your life with all the colors that you give me!

You are a daughter of the Creator of the universe, and I love you and desire for you to be happy and close to me.

Enjoy each moment you have on this Earth because life is a gift, sweetheart. I am with you, longing to see you smile and laugh without fear of the future!

So smile, beautiful one – I love you

Love,
The keeper of your heart

_____

_____

_____

_____

_____

_____

_____

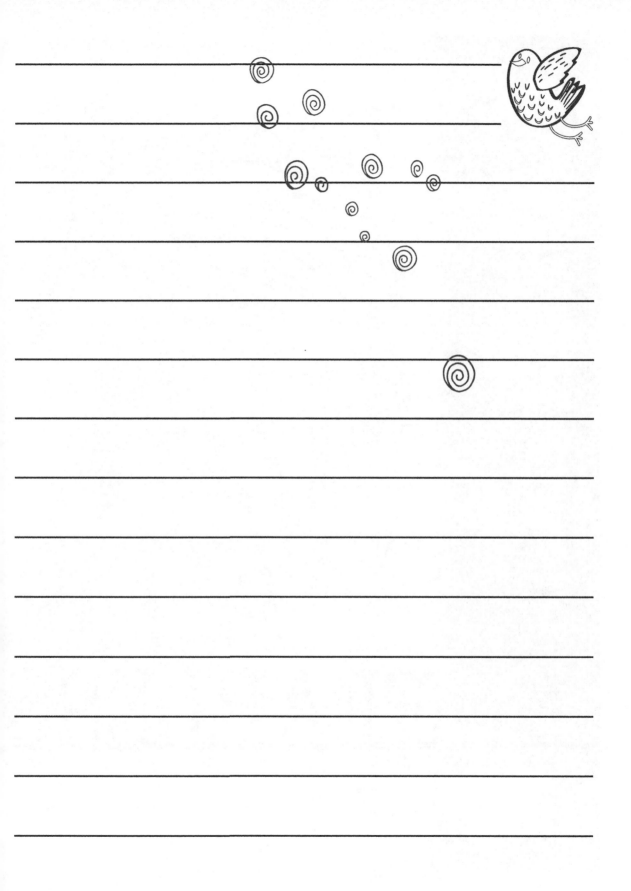

You Are

"Have I not commanded you? Be strong and courageous. Do not be afraid; do not be discouraged, for the Lord your God will be with you wherever you go." Joshua 1:9 (NIV)

FEARLESS

My Brave Girl,

Fear is not of you. Fear is learned from this world. I did not create you to be fearful. I created you to be a fearLESS girl, who doesn't worry, chases her dreams, and has MUCH faith in me.

All this fear and worry that is consuming your mind did not come from me and will never come from me. You picked it up on your journey in this life from watching others be afraid and from events that have happened. Get rid of it! Fear constrains the joy that was given to you on the cross. Fear limits you. Fear can keep you from the amazing plans I have for your life. Fear is false. It's a lie.

The opposite of fear is faith, and faith can move mountains – the obstacles, the sickness, and the messes that are of this world. Faith in my power heals! And I want you to have enough confidence and boldness in me that you practice moving mountains for others and for yourself – through ME!

I don't even want you to fear death. This life is a gift, but the end of this life is only the beginning of eternity with me if you believe in me. Do not worry about how or when you will die. That is all in my hands; you have no control over that and you are not supposed to. Surrender these things that you can't control, and let them go into my hands.

This life will throw you some curveballs. You will get bad news some days. You will not get your way other days. People will disappoint you because they are human, and life isn't always fair. This is a truth in this life. When these things happen, picture yourself wrapping that worry in a box and laying it before me, and then LEAVE IT THERE. I will do what needs to be done with it.

Trust me, my child; trust me and have faith that I will work out ALL things for your good according to my will for your life.

I am worthy of your trust, fearLESS girl.

Love,
The keeper of your heart

"Fear not; you will no longer live in shame. Don't be afraid; there is no more disgrace for you. You will no longer remember the shame of your youth ... For your Creator will be your husband; the Lord of Heaven's Armies is his name! He is your Redeemer, the Holy One of Israel, the God of all the earth."
Isaiah 54:4-5 (NLT)

You are Precious

My Precious One,

Do you know what "precious" means? It means of great value. You, my princess, are so very valuable to me. I know that you have been treated as if you are not of great value. My love, I have seen it all, and it is never my will for you to ever be treated wrongly or looked at as if you are not precious. It pains me to see the world becoming more perverted every day. The way my creation views intimacy has been twisted by the enemy to try to steal the beauty and innocence from my precious daughters.

Beloved, I know how this world has hurt you, and I understand that your mind needs healing. I understand that there have been times where you may have had difficulty valuing your own body. I know everything, and you are still my princess.

Lift up your head, beautiful, and feel comforted that I will heal you and your mind if you stay with me and continue to walk with me.

I will put confidence where there is shame.
I will make the twisted thoughts straight.
I will honor you, uplift you, and help you feel worthy of the best.
I will make you feel clean again, and I will give you a WHITE dress to wear
-- a robe of righteousness.
I will be your husband, and I will value you and treasure you until you see yourself as a spotless bride.

Let the purity of my love make you feel new again!

I hope that as you see my love for you, that you are willing to let me be your husband first, forever. Until I bring into your life your earthly husband, it would make me so proud to see you make decisions that value your body and your soul, and save your body until your wedding day. Oh, how I hope you will say yes! You will not regret it, I can promise you that!

I love you, my precious bride! Now and forever.

Love,
The keeper of your heart

"Jesus said to her, 'I am the resurrection and the life. The one who believes in me will live, even though they die;'"
John 11:25 (NIV)

You Are Heaven Bound

Dear Sweetheart,

Before reading my letters to you, did you have a different view of me? Maybe you pictured me not so loving? Angry? Hard to reach? Far away?

Now that you see that I am not any of those things, are you willing to live your life with me?

My hope is that you believe that I died for you so that you could have a relationship with me, and so that you could be free of the junk that keeps you far away from your Creator. It is my desire for you to understand how much I truly love you and for you to receive this UNCONDITIONAL love.

I can promise you that your life will have so much more meaning and beauty with me by your side. But I am a gentleman, and as much as I love you, I will never force you to love me back. True love is not forceful.

If you choose to accept me as the love of your life, we will have an amazing journey together. I cannot promise you there won't be pain, but I can promise you this – that I will make everything that happens in your life work out for your GOOD. I will use you in mighty ways to display my love and I will talk to you daily, if you take time to listen. I will never leave you, even through death and beyond this Earth to eternity.

You. Are. My. Love.

If you choose me, then all you have to do is truly mean this when you say it: "Jesus, I believe you died for me. I want to have you by my side for the rest of my life. Take my heart and keep it forever, as I accept your loving heart for me today and always."

If you prayed this prayer from your heart, then ALL of HEAVEN is rejoicing over you, my sweet girl!

You are HEAVEN-BOUND!
I promise to keep your heart safe and love you FOREVER! You are mine and I am yours.

As a symbol, write your name in the middle of the heart on the next page as a reminder of who you TRULY are. Keep it in a place where you can see it every day so you don't forget how I see you and who walks with you daily.

Love,
JESUS, the keeper of your heart

P.S. I wanted you to have this book to START our journey together. The end of this book is just the beginning, my love. Talk to me, write to me, draw to me ... I am always with you.

_____

_____

_____

_____

_____

_____

_____

_____

Now that you KNOW who you are, write your name in the middle of this heart and put it on your mirror where you will see it every day!

Show the world that you know who you are and whose you are by taking a selfie with your first name on this page and posting it to The Keeper of My Heart Facebook page (be sure to like the page to see updated posts).

If you prayed and asked Jesus to keep your heart for the first time through this book, please send a message to Ashley@thekeeperofmyheart.com saying you did so, and receive back a special message.

Visit www.thekeeperofmyheart.com to continue to grow in your true identity, and for encouraging blog posts, videos, products, and more.

Made in the USA
Monee, IL
18 March 2022

93144984R00037